SANTA CRUZ
THROUGH TIME

A Journey from Mission Hill to the Monterey Bay

DEBORAH MUTH

MODERN PHOTOGRAPHS BY SIÂN BURCKETT ST. LAURENT

AMERICA
THROUGH
TIME

America Through Time®
An imprint of Sutton Publishing Inc
www.through-time.com
office@through-time.com

First published 2019
Reprinted 2025

ISBN 978-1-63500-091-7

Typeset in Mrs Eaves XL Serif Narrow
Printed and bound in the United States of America

INTRODUCTION

Surrounded by steep mountains, deep gorges and fast-running rivers, the Santa Cruz region in the late 1700s was not an easy place for explorers to reach. The relative isolation had allowed the Ohlone natives to live a peaceful life here for generations by hunting, fishing, gathering edible plants and trading. Explorer Don Gaspar de Portola, sent by Charles III to solidify Spain's claim to Alta California, named the rushing river the San Lorenzo after Saint Lawrence, and the new mission "Missión la Exaltación de la Santa Cruz" (or Holy Cross). Using narrow Indian trails, church padres and fur traders made their way to Santa Cruz, marveling at the vast amounts of natural resources, including the immense Redwood trees.

In 1791, the padres founded Mission Santa Cruz, the twelfth church in the northern California Mission chain. The Spanish government also established a civilian pueblo, the Villa de Branciforte, on the east side of the San Lorenzo River. Under Mexican rule after the War of Independence, the missions were disbanded in 1833, and the assets distributed not to the natives as decreed, but mostly to local administrators and their relatives and friends. Once numbering in the hundreds, by 1839, due to introduced diseases and a changing lifestyle, the native population had shrunk to seventy-one.

With the secession of the former Mexican lands and the admittance of California as the thirty-first state, residents petitioned the newly formed state government for county status. In 1850, the newly seated state legislature designated the region south to the Pajaro River and north to the site of present day Pecadero as Branciforte County, which was changed a short time later to Santa Cruz County (and Pescadero was later added to San Mateo County). Often first drawn to California by the Gold Rush, new arrivals settled in Santa Cruz and built lumber mills, tanneries, paper mills, lime-making facilities, explosive powder works, stage coach lines, railroad lines, gristmills and foundries.

However, around the turn of the century, the promising economic future of Santa Cruz began to change. The inevitable depletion of the tan oaks and easily harvested lumber along with the rise of steam power and electricity led to the relocation of some industries, while new technologies of concrete and dynamite replaced the old products. Increasingly, Santa Cruz turned toward tourism to support the local economy. New facilities such as Fred Swanton's beachside casino and the grand Sea Beach Hotel, as well as more moderately priced accommodations, replaced the early salt-water baths and inexpensive boarding houses. The rise of the automobile and the building of the Glenwood Highway in 1915 also brought more short-term tourists to the area.

The great depression of the 1930s and the entrance of the United States into WWII caused yet another change in the Santa Cruz tourist trade. In the decades following the war, families drove over the re-routed Highway 17 and stopped at new roadside attractions, including Santa's Village, Roaring Camp and Henry Cowell Redwoods State Park. Many new businesses came to Santa Cruz at this time, including Lockheed, Plantronics, Watkins-Johnson, Sylvania Electric, Wrigley's and Lipton. Eagerly anticipated by residents, the founding of the University of California, Santa Cruz in 1965 would bring about bigger changes to the city than could be imagined at the time. Built on the site of the former Cowell Family Ranch, the campus would grow from an initial 652 students to 19,457 students in 2019. Devastating floods in 1955, a series of shocking murder sprees, the closing of most of the major manufacturing facilities, a developing progressive local government and the changing of the downtown business district to a pedestrian friendly mall further influenced the city during this time.

After experiencing past earthquakes, fires, floods, landslides and later even a tsunami, the October 17, 1989, Loma Prieta earthquake inflicted the greatest toll of all on the city. As a result of damage from the 6.9 magnitude jolt, thirty-eight buildings in downtown Santa Cruz alone were demolished, including the first structure built in the downtown, the Flatiron building, and the beloved former County Courthouse-Cooper House. Soon, a new five-story, 119,714-square-foot, mixed-use structure will fill the last vacant spot on Pacific Avenue, replacing the damaged 1899 Williamson and Garrett grocery store, (also the former home of Bookshop Santa Cruz). As technology changes and society shifts happen so quickly, there is no way to predict what Santa Cruz will look like in twenty-five, fifty or 100 years. But by examining the past and understanding those forces that shaped the present, we can better prepare for the future.

AUTHOR'S NOTE ON PHOTOGRAPHS

All photographs used in this book are given full attribution in the caption in brackets except for those labeled [*SBSL*]. These photos are the work of Siân Burckett St. Laurent, who took the majority of the present-day photos. For brevity, I have identified those photo attributions with initials.

1

"O Cruz Ave Spes Unica"
"Hail, thou Cross, our only hope"

In this photo *circa* 1866, the Mission Chapel wing can be seen to the left of the second Holy Cross Church, and at center right is the plaza, the Fallon Hotel, the two-and-a-half story Eagle hotel and the School Street Adobe. [*The Society of California Pioneers*]

Mission and Replica: No known photographs exist of the original Mission Santa Cruz exterior. Existing depictions of the old church are based on building ruins and local recollections. [*The Fine Arts Museums of San Francisco, Oriana Weatherbee Day, "Mission Santa Cruz," Oil on Canvas, 20" X 30," gift of Mrs. Eleanor Martin*] A one-third-size replica of the original Santa Cruz Mission opened to the public in 1932. [*Author*]

INSIDE THE MISSION REPLICA: One of the original artifacts on display from the old mission includes the limestone baptismal font. [*Library of Congress, HABS CAL, 44-SACRU, 1-17, photo by H. Beardsall*] Based on historical research done at the time of construction, the layout and decoration of the chapel closely replicates the original mission church. The motto painted above the outside entrance to the chapel translates to "Hail, thou Cross, our only hope." Originally founded in 1791 on an unknown site near the San Lorenzo River, the padres moved the mission location up the hill the following year due to flooding, and three years later completed the first dedicated church. [*SBSL*]

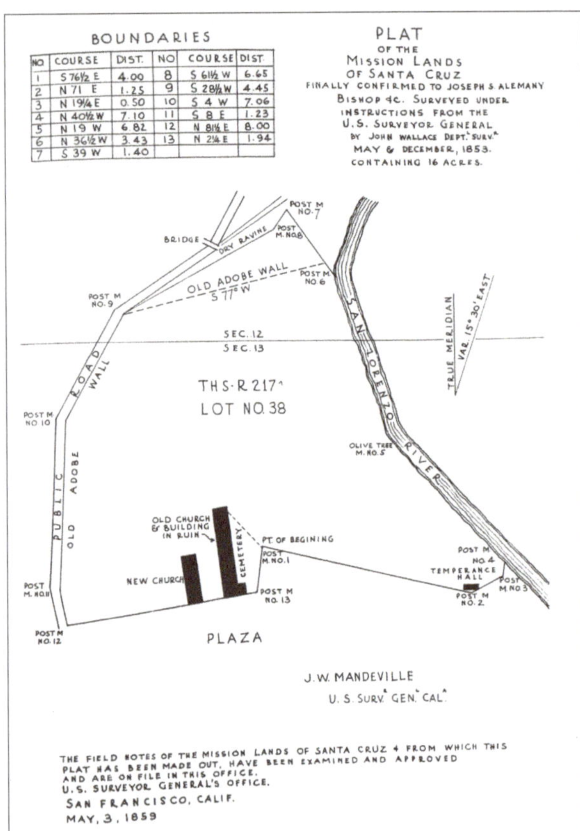

NO	COURSE	DIST.	NO	COURSE	DIST.
1	S 76½ E	4.00	8	S 6½ W	6.65
2	N 71 E	1.25	9	S 28½ W	4.45
3	N 19¾ E	0.50	10	S 4 W	7.06
4	N 40½ W	7.10	11	S 8 E	1.23
5	N 19 W	6.82	12	N 8½ E	8.00
6	N 36½ W	3.43	13	N 2¼ E	1.94
7	S 39 W	1.40			

MISSION MAP AND WALL REMNANT: The original mission lands claimed by the padres spread twenty-eight miles north from the San Lorenzo River to present day Harvey West Park. Church property included vast wheat fields, orchards, vineyards and grazing lands. Secularization started in 1833 and considerably reduced diocese land ownership to eventually only properties around the plaza. The map shown to the left depicts the former mission lands officially conveyed to the Catholic Church in 1859. [*Library of Congress, HABS CAL, 44-SACRU, 1-3*] Recent archaeological research theorizes this remnant of a Mission wall located behind the current Holy Cross Church may have been part of an addition attached to the original chapel that also included a blacksmith shop, wine cellar and distillery. [*SBSL*]

MISSION BURIALS: Originally located on the eastern side of the old adobe church, the mission cemetery grew over time, extending down the hillside. Construction of the new brick church in 1889 made it necessary to remove a portion of the graveyard. The church reburied some of the remains further down the hill and other remains went to the Holy Cross Cemetery in the Live Oak area, located on the outskirts of Santa Cruz. Further grading of the area in 1950 caused more remains to be moved to the same cemetery. [*Library of Congress, HABS CAL,44-SACRU,-20*] In 2016, three bronze plaques containing all the known native names were placed at Holy Cross Cemetery to commemorate the natives reburied there. [*SBSL*]

THE MISSION PLAZA: Many civic, military and philanthropic organizations chose Santa Cruz for the location of their conventions, due to the good weather and easy access by steamer or train, like this Grand Army of the Republic National Encampment of 1886. A newspaper account states, "The entire plaza was canopied with redwood foliage ... beeves [pieces of beef] were barbequed over hot coals." In 1866, a squatter attempted to build a home on a portion of the plaza; however, in short order, the dwelling was torn down by angry citizens and the lumber burned in a celebratory bonfire. [*Special Collections, University Library, University of California Santa Cruz, Historic Photos*] Today, the Mission Plaza is a pleasant city park. [*SBSL*]

SECOND AND THIRD CHURCH: Built in 1857, to replace the old Mission chapel, the new church stood next to the extensively remodeled remains of the old adobe mission, shown to the right. The rock-and-mortar lined irrigation ditch, or *zanja*, seen just behind the boy in the top photo, originally supplied water to the Mission Hill area from the upper High Street area. The top photo was published in 1866. [*Library of Congress, LC-USZ62-26954*] Soon, the wooden church grew too small and a new church was commissioned in 1889 for $35,000. The granite arch was added in 1891 to commemorate the one hundredth anniversary of Mission Santa Cruz. Today, Holy Cross Church continues to be a vital religious presence in the community. [*SBSL*]

CHURCH BUILDINGS: The above photo taken *circa* 1896 depicts the church buildings along High Street. Note that at this time, Highway One did not split High Street. [*Santa Cruz Public Libraries*] At its peak in 1830, the mission had approximately thirty structures, including: spinning rooms; shoemaker and saddle shops; grinding and mill rooms; soap and candle-making sheds; and other outbuildings and living quarters. Wet winters, heavy frosts, inadequate foundations, ground water seepage, earthquakes and the pilfering of the adobe roof tiles and lumber led to the eventual deterioration and collapse of the mission buildings. Present-day church buildings include, left to right: a newer parish hall (built in 1990 after a fire destroyed the old hall), rectory and Holy Cross Church. [*SBSL*]

HOLY CROSS SCHOOL: Situated on the top of Mission Hill, the imposing three-story School of the Holy Cross could be seen from most of Santa Cruz. Founded in 1862 by the Daughters of Charity, the Catholic Girls' School offered day classes and Semester boarding and took in orphans. On this site, the sisters first held school in the old Eagle Hotel, a former adobe building that had also been used as the first government buildings of the newly formed Santa Cruz County. [*Special Collections, University Library, University of California, Santa Cruz, Historic Photos*] The current Holy Cross School, built in 1958, now offers co-ed education classes. The original rock wall built in 1884 can still be seen. [*Author*]

SCHOOL STREET ADOBE: Believed to be the only original remaining example of native housing in the California Mission chain, the School Street Adobe was the last construction in Santa Cruz done under Spanish rule in 1824. It is also the only remaining whole structure from Mission Santa Cruz times. Over the years, the seven-room addition to the original structure underwent extensive remodeling. The 1936 photo above depicts the adobe's last use as a duplex before being sold to the State of California in 1957. [*Library of Congress, HABS CAL, 44-SACRU, 1-18, photo by Robert Kerrigan*] In 1991, the adobe was restored and opened as a State Park to represent typical housing of native mission workers and the post-secularization inhabitants. [*SBSL*]

Mission Hill Structures: Built in 1864, on the site of the first jail, and constructed of locally quarried granite, the second Santa Cruz jail contained only four cells. Three Santa Cruz High graduates are identified in this 1893 photo: Mabel Lincoln, Helen Younger and Adelaide Becker. The jail stood in the vicinity of the present Holy Cross Church parking lot. When the jail was torn down in 1906, many of the granite blocks were reused for local gravestones. [*Santa Cruz Museum of Art and History*] With the closing of both the girls' and boys' schools, the diocese built a new School of the Holy Cross in 1932, which was closed in 1970 due to declining enrollment. [*SBSL*]

SYLVAR STREET RESIDENCES: Thought to be the oldest frame-built house in Santa Cruz, Francisco Alzina built this modest house in the 1850s to replace the adobe home of his in-laws. Alzina, the first sheriff of Santa Cruz County, and his wife, Carlotta Gonzalez Alzina, raised fourteen children here. [*Santa Cruz Museum of Art and History*] Sometime in the late 1880s, Henry Willey constructed a family home, seen left in the bottom photo next the Alzina home. Later, the Daughters of Charity occupied the Willey home for a time as a convent house. [*SBSL*]

WATCH SANTA CRUZ GROW

The Town Clock Park at the head of Pacific Avenue and Mission and Front streets provides an open-air community gathering place. [*Author*]

On the "Flat": Having run out of room for expansion on Mission Plaza, new construction began on the former mission agricultural fields below. Elihu Anthony constructed the first commercial building, a modest wood-frame store seen in the lower left of this photo *circa* 1865. Located further down the street were: Zebulon Sprague's Gun Shop, the Santa Cruz House and the Franklin House (both hotels), saloons and Chinese laundries. [*Santa Cruz Museum of Art and History*] Trees planted after the 1989 earthquake provide an attractive canopy, but greatly obscure building views. [*SBSL*]

LATER DOWNTOWN VIEWS: Standing prominently at the head of the town's two main streets for 130 years, the Flatiron building housed many businesses over the years since its completion in 1860. The second floor served as the County Courthouse from 1860 to 1864. A "Liberty Flag Pole" can be seen in the above photo, center front. Patriotic businesses vied with each other to have the tallest mast. From this photo *circa* 1880, streetcar lines and the Pacific Ocean House can also be seen to the right. [*Ronnie Trubek*] Heavily damaged in the 1989 earthquake, the Flatiron building was demolished and replaced by the present building. [*SBSL*]

VIEW UP MISSION STREET: In this photo from 1866, the St. Charles Hotel can be seen to the extreme right with the Otto Diesing Brewery adjacent to the left. The brewery produced about 200 barrels of beer a week and used caves dug into the hillside to store malt and barley. The Diesing family lived above the brewery. Beyond the brewery stood the post office and then Temperance Hall, a large public meeting place. Standing at the top of the hill was the imposing Mission Hill School, then to the left a blacksmith shop and barbershop. [*California History Room, California State Library, Sacramento, California*] Today only the original Mission Hill School steps and retaining wall remain. [*SBSL*]

CLOSE-UP MISSION STREET: Above, the close-up photograph shows the businesses along the north side of the street in greater detail. Temperance Hall once stood at the level of School Street above, but was later dug out and lowered to the level of Mission Street. [*Santa Cruz Museum of Art and History*] Today, there are only a few businesses located on the north side of the street, partially due to a lack of space. In 1862, the *Santa Cruz Sentinel* reported thirty feet of the bluff near the present-day intersection of North Pacific and Mission streets slid to the street below due to heavy rains. [*SBSL*]

DOWNTOWN BUSINESSES: In an unusual pose for the time (note the expression of the little boy near the center), George Hastings, on the far right, stands in front of his store located on Pacific Avenue (*circa* 1900). In addition to selling jewelry, musical instruments and eyeglasses, he taught music lessons, tuned pianos and organized the first local musicians' union. Known as "Professor" Hastings he conducted and managed two prominent local bands, the 50-piece Santa Cruz Beach Band and the Brownie Orchestra for children. [*Santa Cruz Museum of Art and History*] Another victim of the 1989 earthquake, the 1873-built Pray Building (home to the Hasting's store), was demolished and replaced with the modern building shown in the bottom photo. [*Author*]

CALVARY EPISCOPAL CHURCH: The oldest church building in Santa Cruz still being used for its original use, Calvary recently celebrated its 150th anniversary of Episcopal services in 2015. After meeting in several other locations, construction began on the gothic-revival style church in 1864; however, it took a few years to complete the building and grounds. [*Calvary Episcopal Church*] Still a thriving parish church, the members remain committed to the church motto of "respect the dignity of every human being" and outreach to the homeless and needy. [*SBSL*]

DOWNTOWN DEVELOPMENT: These similar views of north Pacific Avenue (top photo *circa* 1895) illustrate the change from buggy and streetcar to automobile and power lines. Both views look north toward the present town clock site. In the upper photo, Mission Hill, the School Street Adobe and the spire of Holy Cross Church can be seen at top. On the left-hand side of the street near the corner is the Pacific Ocean House. Taken approximately twenty-five years later, the west side of the Flatiron building can be seen at the head of Pacific Avenue and Front Street. [*Santa Cruz Museum of Art and History*]

HEATH AND BYRNE HARDWARE STORE: Lucien "Tink" Heath built his hardware store on the south side of Church Street and Pacific Avenue in 1883. He and his partner, Charles Byrne, specialized in stoves, and the rear of the business housed tinsmiths, tinkers and sheet metal workers. In 1897, the business became the Byrne Brothers. In the above photo, the building is shown decorated for the 4th of July. The photo below depicts a shipment of stoves for the Byrne Brothers moved by the Seidlinger Transfer Company. [*Santa Cruz Museum of Art and History*]

GERMANIA HOTEL.

—

THE UNDERSIGNED HAVING PUR-
chased the interest of Daniel Wente,
in the Railroad House, on Front street,
have refitted, refurnished and renovated
the same, and will open it under the
name of the

GERMANIA HOTEL.

On Monday, November 1st.

By strict attention to business they hope
to merit a share of public patronage.

The Bar is stocked with the best
brands of wines, liquors and cigars.

Meals,   :   :   :   :   :   :   25 cts
Lodgings,   :   :   :   :   :   25 cts
Board and lodging per day,   : $1 00
Board and lodging per week, :   5 00
Board per week,   :   :   :   :   4 00
   Oct. 30, tf. CHARLES WEBER & CO.

THE GERMANIA HOTEL: Built in 1877 by Robert Whidden, the original foundation used butt logs milled from his sawmill in today's Granite Creek-Scotts Valley area and hauled to Santa Cruz via ox team. A few years later, Frank Pratcher and Charles Weber moved their Germania Hotel from Front and Cooper Streets to the Vine Street (now Locust and Cedar Street) location. In 1899, the Germania House became the Santa Cruz Hotel. (A side view of the hotel can be seen on page 25.) [*Santa Cruz Museum of Art and History*] Meals and lodging rates varied, as shown in this 1874 newspaper advertisement. [*Author*]

THE SANTA CRUZ HOTEL: The Hotel Santa Cruz's Crown Room was a popular 1950s and 1960s downtown institution known for its formal portraits of the Miss California Pageant winners lining the walls, double martinis and savory Italian food. [*Santa Cruz Museum of Art and History*] The building currently houses Planet Fresh Burritos and the Red Restaurant and Bar. [*SBSL*]

THE PACIFIC OCEAN HOUSE: Located on the west side of Pacific Avenue opposite the Flatiron building, this well-known resort hotel welcomed the wealthy and famous to Santa Cruz for over forty years. The three-story, 150-room hotel featured a front veranda with rocking chairs, an elegant bar, a billiards room and extensive gardens in the rear. A corner room housed the first bank in Santa Cruz. In later years the hotel became a boarding house and the last sections were torn down in 1966. [*Santa Cruz Museum of Art and History*]

PACIFIC OCEAN HOUSE TREE: This immense Black Walnut tree fronting Cedar Street is the last remnant of the extensive gardens of the Pacific Ocean House. The gardens stretched from behind the hotel on Pacific Avenue to Cedar Street and included extensive paths with flowers, shrubs, trees, a fishpond and a teahouse. [*Santa Cruz Museum of Art and History*] In 1995, arborists observed fungus growing on the tree that led to a recommendation for removal. Due to the public outcry, a "crown restoration" procedure was attempted to allow the tree to create a new, less-heavy branching structure. Although somewhat odd looking close up, the tree has generated much new growth and remains a beloved link to past Santa Cruz history. [*SBSL*]

CORNER OF WALNUT AND PACIFIC: Moved from Mission and Pacific in 1927 by F. A. Hihn, this building provided a grocery store to the nearby developing residential neighborhood. In 1920, the New Santa Cruz Theatre replaced the store. The slogan painted on the side of the building for MJB Coffee in this 1917 photo was part of an early ad campaign to attract attention for the MJB brand. The phrase, "Why?" had no particular meaning, other than to attract consumer attention and encourage speculation. [*Santa Cruz Museum of Art and History*] Floodwaters saturated the theatre in 1956 and despite community objections it closed for good to be remodeled into other businesses. Today, the adjacent Harris Brothers building still stands. [*SBSL*]

THE HINDS HOUSE: Built in 1888 for Sarah and Alfred Hinds, this three-story, 6,000-square-foot Stick-Eastlake-style home [seen left] reportedly contains the first electric light in Santa Cruz. The H. E. Irish house can be seen to the far right of the photo. [*Santa Cruz Museum of Art and History*] Restored in 1981, the house is now an extended-stay hotel. All the stairs shown in the photo above that lead from above the hill to the street below have been closed off or removed. One set of stairs, not seen to the right, still links Walnut Street to Towne Terrace. [*SBSL*]

LADIES' FASHION: In 1892, Samuel Leask and John Johnston purchased the Seaside Store and through their efforts it became a successful business. In 1896 Leask bought out his partner and in 1906 relocated the store to the corner of Church and Pacific Avenue, shown here in this 1909 photo. Over the next decades, he remodeled and expanded the department store. In 1988, the Gottschalk's Department Store firm bought the Leask's Store chain, but sadly parts of the Santa Cruz store collapsed in the 1989 earthquake and the store was demolished shortly thereafter. Today, the Cinema 9 complex occupies the old store site. [*Special Collections, University Library, University of California, Santa Cruz, Historic Photos*] Below, currently the store Urban Outfitters occupies a portion of the former Leask's. [*SBSL*]

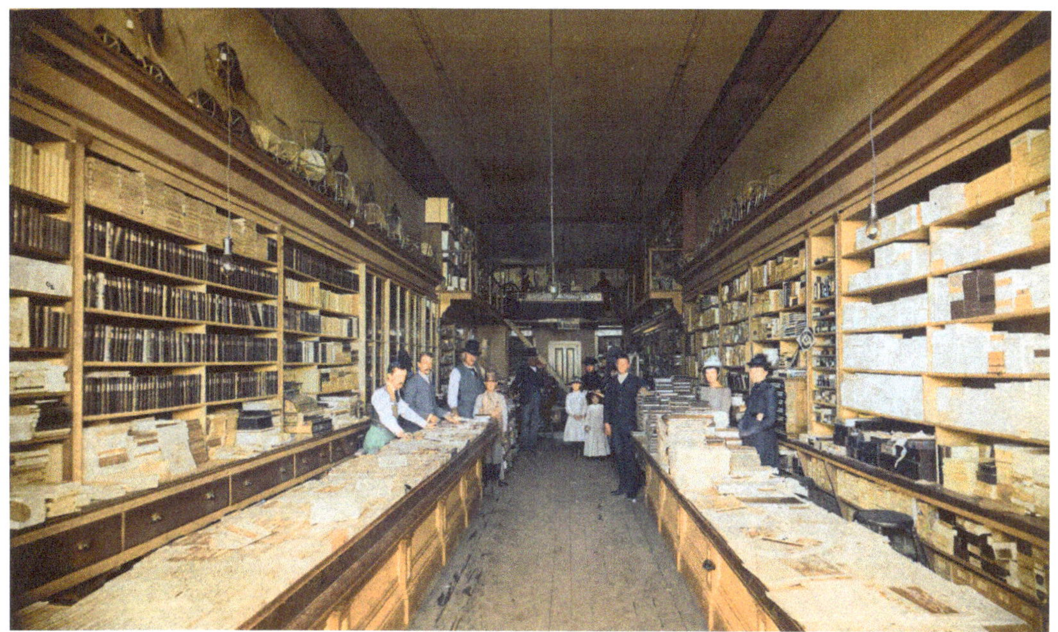

MORE DOWNTOWN BUSINESSES: Photographed in 1890, the H. E. Irish store sold a variety of goods including new and used books, toys, stationary and fishing tackle. In later years they also carried phonographs and records. Today the present-day specialty shops Nectar and Camouflage occupy the former H. E. Irish store site. [*Santa Cruz Museum of Art and History*] A downtown institution, Atlantis Fantasyworld, sells comic books, toys and memorabilia. Pictured left to right: Nathan Brand, owner Jose Ferrara and Trisha Wolfe. The original store location was featured in the 1987 cult film *The Lost Boys*, filmed in Santa Cruz. [*SBSL*]

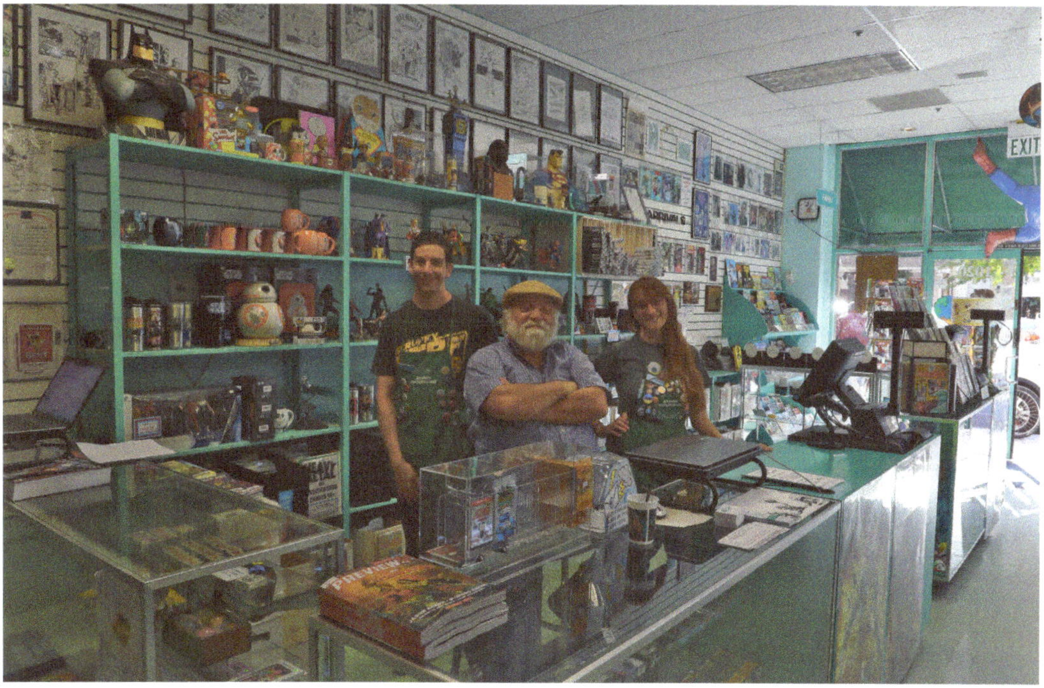

CORNER OF LOCUST AND PACIFIC: This early photo depicts a dirt road, horse-drawn buggies and residences just off Pacific Avenue. The building to the right dates from 1866 and was demolished in 1910 for the present building. [*Santa Cruz Museum of Art and History*] The well-known local architect William Weeks designed The People's Bank building that later became a Wells Fargo Bank branch, then Integrand Design and now the SockShop and Shoe Company. [*SBSL*]

THE DOWNTOWN FARMER'S MARKET: Restricted to food items produced locally, farmers backed their wagons up the east side of Front Street between Cooper Street and Soquel Avenue to sell their wares. Later, as shown in this photo from 1915, the market moved further down Front Street to the west side. [*Santa Cruz Museum of Art and History*] A local institution started in 1990, the year-round downtown Farmer's Market at Cedar and Lincoln Streets sells a wide variety of local organic produce and other products. Food trucks, live music and the meeting of friends contribute to the festive atmosphere. [*SBSL*]

PACIFIC AVENUE: This 1920 view of Pacific Avenue looking north (just south of Soquel) shows a number of bygone downtown businesses. The streetcar track branching off to the right was to the Twin Lakes-Capitola line. In 1904, a former feed store became the 700-seat Unique Theater. Three years later, Mack and Cora Belle Swain purchased the theater and it became Swain's Theater. In 1910, the Swains left Santa Cruz for Hollywood and the theater name reverted back to the Unique. Mack Swain most notably appeared in Charlie Chaplin's 1925 movie *The Gold Rush*. The Unique closed in 1936, the same year the Del Mar Theater opened. [*Santa Cruz Museum of Art and History*]

Santa Cruz Film History: The movie posters date this photo of the Grand Theatre from 1915. The theatre was located on Pacific Avenue. [*Santa Cruz Museum of Art and History*] Recognized early on as a talented actress at Santa Cruz High School, Eliza Susan (known as ZaSu, and correctly pronounced "Say Zoo") Pitts lived her early years in the family home located next to the current Nickelodeon Theatre on Lincoln Street. She was "discovered" in 1917 and went on have a highly successful career in films. One of her most famous role was that of "Tina," the lead female role in *Greed*, directed by Erich Von Stroheim. [*SBSL*]

THE DEL MAR THEATRE: Built in 1936 as a result of rising theater patronage, the Del Mar was Santa Cruz's first modern theater. The venue had 950 general admission seats, 350 balcony seats, 200 loge seats, a stage, a twenty-five-piece orchestra pit, modern projection faculties and ten theater attendants per show. [*Santa Cruz Museum of Art and History*] Over the years, the theater's condition deteriorated and it was sectioned off into four separate screens. Facing permanent closure in 1999, the Santa Cruz Redevelopment Agency purchased the facility and provided the funds for refurbishment. Landmark Theatres has operated the movie house since 2015. [*SBSL*]

THE ST. GEORGE HOTEL: Built by Anson Hotaling in 1893, the first hotel on this site was destroyed by fire in 1894 and rebuilt shortly thereafter. The elegant interior featured a marble staircase and the first hydraulic elevator in the county. The exterior was remodeled in 1929 to the Spanish-Colonial-Revival style shown in the upper photograph. The delicate latticework walls and ceiling of the Palm Room would later become The Catalyst, a downtown landmark of the 1960s. [*Santa Cruz Public Libraries*] Heavily damaged by both the 1989 earthquake and a subsequent fire, the St. George was demolished and later reconstructed in 1992. Below, the current back view of the hotel is shown as trees obstruct the front view. [*SBSL*]

THE HOTEL PALOMAR: It was Andy Balich, real estate broker and promoter, who coined the phrase "Santa Cruz … always growing." Designed by architect William Weeks, Balich and his partners opened the hotel in 1929. When completed, it was the county's first "skyscraper" at seven stories. Built at a cost of around $600,000, the hotel had 100 rooms, each with its own bathroom, a 200-person capacity ballroom, a 100-seat meeting room and two elevators. In the street view photo below, the hotel can be seen in the middle of the block with the New Santa Cruz Theatre to the far left and the Odd Fellows Building just beyond the hotel. [*Santa Cruz Museum of Art and History*]

More Hotel Palomar: In 1932, Betty and Benny Fox, a brother-sister team, staged a marathon dancing and acrobatic act on a 50-foot pole with a 30-inch platform placed on top of the roof of the hotel for three days and two nights. [*Santa Cruz Museum of Art and History*] Now renamed the Palomar Inn, the hotel underwent extensive remodeling and retrofitting just shortly before the 1989 earthquake. Fortunately, the building only sustained minor damage from the earthquake, although there was a reported mile of short wall cracks that were repaired with special epoxy glue. Busts of Spanish explorers adorn the top floor of the building. [*SBSL*]

SANTA CRUZ'S CHINATOWNS: Four distinct Chinatowns developed over time in Santa Cruz. The third, Birkenseer's Chinatown (pictured above), roughly occupied the area running south-east along Front Street, starting from Cooper Street to Soquel Avenue and east to the San Lorenzo River, from around 1900. The street shown in the photo is today a pedestrian path. Shown below is a photograph of the members of the Chinese Christian Mission in Santa Cruz taken roughly the same time. Members met weekly to study the Bible and learn to read and speak English. [*Santa Cruz Museum of Art and History*]

CHINESE TEMPLE AND REDEVELOPMENT: The interior of the Chee Kong Tong Temple combined elements of Christianity (see the poster of the Ten Commandments posted on the wall) with elements of Chinese religious practice. The decorations shown in the photo appear to be for a New Year's celebration. [*Santa Cruz Museum of Art and History*] By 1952, only one of the homes in Birkenseer's Chinatown remained occupied and the flood of 1955 finally forced those residents to leave their home. Shortly thereafter, the area underwent redevelopment. [*Author*]

WWI MEMORIAL: In the photo above, the Santa Cruz WWI Memorial can be seen directly in front of a newly remodeled four-room bungalow. As a 1934 demonstration project, the Santa Cruz Better Housing Campaign moved an old building from the defunct Schuette Mattress Works to the Post Office-Town Plaza area and completely remodeled the structure. When rebuilt, the bungalow and a plot of land were raffled off to a lucky winner. [*Special Collections, University Library, University of California Santa Cruz, Historic Photos*] Installed in 1928, the WWI memorial contains the names of forty-five war veterans, including one female Red Cross Nurse. [*SBSL*]

DOWNTOWN EVENTS: In this extraordinary photograph from 1903 (above), then President Teddy Roosevelt speaks to the crowd on Pacific Avenue standing from a carriage (right). (Look for the baby being held up to the window.) T. R. came to Santa Cruz to visit the Big Trees Grove in Felton and afterward stated, "We should keep the trees as we should keep great stretches of the wildernesses as a heritage for our children ... to preserve them for beauty ... for the sake of the nation hereafter." [*California History Room, California State Library, Sacramento, California*] In the lower photo, the 2018 Santa Cruz Pride Parade ends the annual procession down Pacific Avenue at Cathcart Street. [*Author*]

COUNTY BANK: In 1895, County Bank directors commissioned the building of a new renaissance revival style bank headquarters built on the former site of a saloon destroyed in the 1894 downtown fire (seen above). [*Special Collections, University Library, University of California Santa Cruz, Historic Photos*] Remodeling in 1910 changed the original appearance of the building to the façade shown in the downtown parade photo below. Once the county's largest bank with the most branches and customers, the original County Bank ceased operations in 1987. [*Santa Cruz Museum of Art and History*]

COUNTY BANK BUILDING RESURRECTED: Badly damaged by the 1989 earthquake, local debate split between saving the County Bank building and tearing it down completely. Ultimately, the new owner, Barry Swenson Builders, incorporated two of the original exterior walls into the new building. In the photo to the right, an observer watches the construction progress. The old Gottschalk's Department Store destroyed by the 1989 earthquake can be seen in the background. [*Santa Cruz Public Libraries*] Now restored and remodeled, the former bank building houses a variety of businesses. [*SBSL*]

FIRE AND FLOOD: Both natural and man-made disasters, including flooding from the San Lorenzo River, earthquakes and major fires, continue to shape Santa Cruz. Early recorded earthquakes damaged both the Mission Hill area and downtown buildings, while a major fire of 1894 (the results shown above) gutted the Cooper Street Court House and destroyed first Chinatown and other businesses located on Front Street. As a result of widespread flooding in 1955, the US Army Corps of Engineers designed extensive flood levees that were built by Granite Construction in 1959. The photo below with the Beach Boardwalk's Giant Dipper Roller Coaster in the background records one of the many floods to inundate the Beach Flats lowlands. [*Santa Cruz Museum of Art and History*]

1989 Earthquake and Aftermath: The 1989 earthquake lasted only fifteen seconds in duration but resulted in the death of six people, 3,000 people homeless and over one billion dollars in property damage. Beloved landmarks, thirty-eight in all, including the historic Flat-Iron Building and the former Court House-Cooper House, were demolished, leaving a hole in the ground and in the hearts of many Santa Cruz residents. Ford's Department Store, the bottom floor shown above, was one of the many casualties of the earthquake. [*Wendy Brannan*] In 1999, the collapsed department store building was demolished and replaced the following year by the five-story, 86,000-square-foot University Town Center. [*SBSL*]

· WELCOME TO DOWNTOWN: Erected in 1921 and located on Ocean at Plymouth streets, the gateway arch welcomed automobile visitors to Santa Cruz. On the reverse was written, "Come Again! You are Welcome!" [*Santa Cruz Museum of Art and History*] Echoing the same welcoming sentiments, the 36-foot long, 25-feet high and eight-foot-wide sign directs visitors to use River Street to downtown Santa Cruz. Built at a cost of $83,000, the controversial landmark seems to invoke either a "love" or "hate" emotion in residents. [*SBSL*]

3

Where Every Day is Summer

Circa 1890 view of the Santa Cruz beach. Note the steam-powered merry-go-round shown at the far left of the photo. [*Santa Cruz Museum of Art and History*]

VISITING SANTA CRUZ: Although popular in Europe for some time, the practice of open salt-water bathing did not catch on Santa Cruz due to the frigid waters of the Monterey Bay. In the early 1860's bathhouses such as Liddell's Long Branch Baths and John Librandt's Dolphin Baths attracted patrons with heated salt-water baths, swimming tanks, dance pavilions and other amusements. Summer visitors came from the sweltering inland valleys and generally stayed a few weeks or more. [*California History Room, California State Library, Sacramento, California*] Today's beach activities have changed to more active forms of recreation. [*SBSL*]

THE FIRST AND SECOND CASINO: In 1903, tireless Santa Cruz promoter Fred Swanton acquired the former Miller-Leibbrandt Plunge and Bathhouse properties. The next year, he opened his grand Moorish-style Neptune Casino, complete with nineteen onion-shaped domes, seen in the photo above. Unfortunately, an early-morning fire burned the new casino to the ground, but Swanton quickly built a new casino in 1907. Swanton later lost the Boardwalk property in 1915 to foreclosure, but later went on to become mayor of Santa Cruz. [*Santa Cruz Museum of Art and History*] Shown below is the current side view of the much-remodeled second casino and beach. [*SBSL*]

THE BOARDWALK PROMENADE: In the early part of the 1900s, vacationers dressed in more formal attire than today. Ladies apparel included a long skirt or dress with a hat, parasol and gloves while gentlemen were expected to wear a coat and tie, even on the beach. Bathing suits of the time consisted of two-piece wool garments with stockings, slippers and caps for women and a modified long-john style of suit for men. Promoter Fred Swanton coined the phrases, "Where it's Summer Every day" and "Santa Cruz—Never a Dull Moment" to attract visitors to Santa Cruz and the Boardwalk. [*California History Room, California State Library, Sacramento, California*] Below, the Boardwalk promenade today. [*SBSL*]

BEACHSIDE BOARDWALK: The rebuilt Boardwalk of 1907 included: a casino (which at the time meant a building used for social functions), a combination theater-ballroom able to hold up to 2,500 patrons, a restaurant, an 84-foot serving bar made of Honduras mahogany, a penny arcade and an ice-cream parlor. The ballroom featured a bandstand, wooden dance floor and twelve upper-level boxes. The Sea Beach Hotel can be seen to the left with the Natatorium to the right in this 1908 photo. [*Sourisseau Academy for State and Local History, San José State University, San José, California*] Shown below is a present-day view with Cap'n Jack Flint's Pirate Ship ride to the right. [*SBSL*]

The Looff Carousel: Built by Charles Looff and installed at the Boardwalk in 1911, the seventy-three horses and two chariots of the elaborately carved carousel continue to delight all ages. The carousel is one of a few left in the United States to feature a working ring-toss. Three organs supply the music to the ride, the original 1864 Ruth and Sohn band organ, a Wurlitzer 165 band organ and a smaller Wurlitzer 146 organ. [*Santa Cruz Beach Boardwalk Archives*] The National Park Service designated the Carousel and the Giant Dipper Roller-coaster as national landmarks in 1987. [*SBSL*]

THE NATATORIUM-PLUNGE: Built to replace the original plunge pool destroyed in the 1906 fire, Swanton constructed his new Natatorium larger and more impressive than the original. The elaborate building contained two pools, an "L" shaped 65-feet-by-135-feet pool, and a smaller pool at 30-feet by 60-feet. Both were heated to a comfortable eighty-three degrees with fresh salt-water brought in daily from a pipe located at the end of the Boardwalk's Pleasure Pier. [*Santa Cruz Beach Boardwalk Archives*] In 1962, due to economic reasons, the Plunge was closed, drained and replaced with the present 18-hole Buccaneer Bay Mini Golf Course. [*SBSL*]

INSIDE THE PLUNGE: In the early years of the Natatorium, few people knew how to swim, so the Boardwalk brought in famous swimmers Arthur Cavill from Australia and Duke Kahanamoku from Hawaii to teach swimming. [*California History Room, California State Library, Sacramento, California*] Later under the direction of Skip Littlefield, extravagant water shows were held at the Plunge from 1927 to 1945. Shown above, Don Patterson, known as the "Mighty Bosco," supports four other performers while hanging upside down from a rope attached to the rafters. He was also the star of the "Stratosphere Dive," the outdoors "Slide for Life" and the "Fire Slide for Life." [*Santa Cruz Beach Boardwalk Archives*]

THE PLUNGE TODAY: Elaborate nautical decorations, including a lighthouse and a rope-climbing pirate, now decorate the mini-golf course; however, the original domed ceiling of the old plunge can still be seen. An aquarium housing alligators, seals, otters and tanks of rare fish once stood next to the Natatorium. Upstairs, the second story of the mini-golf features a display of popular bygone arcade machines. [*SBSL*]

 Recognizing the need for inexpensive vacation rentals, Fred Swanton built 200 wood and canvas structures opposite the casino on the former Dolphin baseball field. In 1907, wood frame bungalows replaced the canvas tents. The bungalows varied in size from one to four rooms with rental rates ranging from $5.00 to $25.00 per week. Built in 1911, the three-story, 329-room hotel Casa Del Rey (Home of the King) replaced the cottages. A covered walkway connected the hotel to the casino. During World War II, the hotel housed naval war patients and in 1960 it became a retirement home. It was demolished shortly after the 1989 earthquake, due to extensive damage. [*Santa Cruz Museum of Art and History*]

THE BEACH TRAIN: Utilizing idle commuter cars on Sundays and holidays, the Southern Pacific Railroad's Sun Tan Special carried an estimated 3,500 people from around the Bay Area to Santa Cruz each operating day. The train service started in 1927 and ran until 1959, except for the war years 1941 through 1947. In the photo above, the soot-stained bridge between the Casa del Rey hotel and the Casino can be seen. [*Santa Cruz Public Libraries*] Now taking passengers from Roaring Camp in Felton (next to the Henry Cowell State Park) to the Boardwalk, the Big Trees and Pacific Railroad operates between April and September. [*SBSL*]

BOARDWALK CONCESSIONS: For thirty-one years until 1948, Henry Schwab Miller or "Hot Dog" Miller as he was known, sold hot dogs at the Boardwalk. His first stand located, near the entrance to the Plunge, sold hot dogs, hamburgers and waffles to hungry customers. Later he went on to open a beer garden near the present Giant Dipper site and a second hot dog stand. A genial and well-liked man, in a newspaper interview he estimated he sold over fifteen million sausages at his Boardwalk stands. [*Special Collections, University Library, University of California, Santa Cruz, Historic Photos*] Today, Miller's Hot Dogs has been replaced by the souvenir and gift store, Sun Shops. [*SBSL*]

THE GIANT DIPPER:

Designed by Frank Prior and Frederick Church and built by Arthur Looff, the now iconic rollercoaster opened in 1924. The heart-pounding ride lasts one minute and fifty-two seconds with speeds up to fifty-five miles per hour and heights up to seventy feet all on a half-mile of thundering wooden tracks. On opening day, the line for the ride stretched two hundred feet before opening and riders paid just fifteen-cents. [*Santa Cruz Beach Boardwalk Archives*] In the present-day photo shown below, not many changes are noticeable. Surprisingly, the original rollercoaster cars were square metal boxes with no seat belts or bars. Today the cars have lockable safety restraints and the coaster features other safety devices. [*SBSL*]

WHARF ENTRANCE: The above *circa* 1890's photo depicting the intersection of today's S. Pacific Avenue and Beach Street captures the Sea Foam Hotel front-left, the back of the Sea Beach Hotel behind the hotel, a horse-drawn streetcar pulling out of view to the right and the Railroad Wharf to the right. [*Special Collections, University Library, University of California, Santa Cruz, Historical Photos*] With a recently added traffic roundabout in front of the Municipal Wharf, today's view bears little resemblance the photo taken more than 100 years ago. [*SBSL*]

THE SEA BEACH HOTEL: Over the years, the Sea Beach Hotel attracted many wealthy and famous guests of the time and also hosted dances, conventions and other social gatherings. The hotel's heyday occurred in 1886 when it re-opened under new management as the Sea Beach Hotel. The newly remodeled guest rooms each had a marble bathroom, closet, electric lights, a fireplace and a telephone. Outside the extensive gardens featured rare and beautiful plants. Tragically, an early morning fire destroyed the hotel in 1912. [*Santa Cruz Public Libraries*] Shown below, the Casa Blanca Inn and Restaurant stands roughly where the Sea Beach Hotel was located. [*SBSL*]

Entrance to the Wharf: The first "wharf" built in Santa Cruz was an incline gravity chute built by Elihu Anthony off present day West Cliff Drive to transport sacks of potatoes onto ships bound for San Francisco. A rising demand for lime led to the construction of the Davis and Jordan Wharf in 1849, which later became known as the Cowell Wharf. The Railroad Wharf depicted in the photo above allowed local businesses easier movement of goods. This wharf stood until 1922. [*Museum of Art and History*] Below, tourists and locals alike frequent the wharf and beach area for its many attractions, including the Monterey Bay National Marine Sanctuary Exploration Center built in 2012. [*SBSL*]

THE MUNICIPAL WHARF: With the voter's approval of a $172,000 bond in 1913 construction began on a 2,745-foot wharf with 2,043 specially selected 70-foot Douglas fir pilings. The creosote treated pilings were drive into the ocean floor twenty-one feet through layers of added sand and clay to rest in a five-foot bed of gravel. Built to encourage fishing and shipping interests the city installed warehouses, faculties for commercial fishermen and railroad tracks down one side of the wharf. In 1938 the city removed the tracks. [*Santa Cruz Museum of Art and History*] Today both residents and tourists alike enjoy the restaurants, shops, sport fishing and a resident colony of sea lions located at the wharf. [*SBSL*]

THE LYNCH HOUSE: In 1877, pioneer businessman Frederick Lynch built this elegant Italianate-style home for his family. In 1909, his widow leased the house to licensed nurse Mary Jane Hanly for use as a Sanitarium. Seeing the need for a modern hospital after the 1918 influenza epidemic, she built Hanly Hospital adjacent to the Sanitarium in 1923. [*Corbett Wright*] After her death, the hospital became Sisters Hospital, run by Sisters from the Adrian Dominican order. In later years, the Lynch house faced an uncertain future until 2006 when CW Land Consultants converted the stately home into the West Cliff Inn. [*SBSL*]

4

"Sine Praejudicio"
"Without Prejudice"

Part of a collaborative program between the City of Santa Cruz and Uber Technologies, Inc., electric pedal assist bikes shown here in front of the Santa Cruz City Hall await the next customers. [*SBSL*]

MISSION STREET TUNNEL: Railroad owners used imported Cornish Miners rather than Chinese workers to build the 939-feet narrow gauge railway tunnel in 1876 due to local prejudice at the time. [*Santa Cruz Public Libraries*] The tunnel remains part of an active rail line maintained by Felton's Big Trees, Santa Cruz and Pacific Railroad and is the oldest tunnel still in use in Santa Cruz. [*SBSL*]

RAILROAD DEPOTS: Early railroad passengers to Santa Cruz passed through the Mission Street tunnel and disembarked at a depot located near the present-day intersection of Chestnut and Union Streets. Facilities there included a passenger terminal, a car-house, an engine house, a freight house and a locomotive turntable. In 1892 under new ownership the South Pacific Coast Railroad moved the station and freight yard south to Chestnut Street. The photo below depicts an early locomotive and crew at the Chestnut Street depot now known as the Union Depot. [*Santa Cruz Museum of Art and History*]

THE UNION DEPOT: Above, a large crowd attends the send-off of World War One recruits from Union Depot. [*Santa Cruz Public Libraries*] With the running of the last "Suntan Special" train in 1959, railroad traffic in Santa Cruz became freight only until the Santa Cruz, Big Trees and Pacific Railroad began operating an excursion line from Felton. In 2005, the city of Santa Cruz opened Depot Park, a seven-acre public recreational space on the site of the former Union Depot. Shown below, a former 1918 American Railway Express Agency freight building from the depot has been remodeled into public restrooms for the park. [*SBSL*]

THE SOQUEL AVENUE BRIDGE: Local newspaper accounts first mention a pedestrian bridge crossing the San Lorenzo River at Soquel Avenue in 1864. Generally high-wheeled wagons were able to safely cross the shallow river, except during the rainy season. Increasing population caused the 1874 building of a new eight-hundred-foot-long bridge with five hundred and thirty feet of covered roadway. [*Library of Congress HABS CAL, 44-SACRU, 2-2*] Increasing automobile traffic forced the replacement of the old wooden bridge in 1921 with a concrete and steel structure, later widened in 1967. Although repaired in 1984 due to storm damage, the bridge was completely replaced in 1999 at a cost of eleven million dollars to meet current earthquake standards. [*SBSL*]

The Water Street Bridge: A total of six bridges currently span the San Lorenzo River in Santa Cruz. The Water Street Bridge also started out as a footbridge in 1866, but after two years was washed away by floodwaters. Due to storm damage, new bridges were built in 1868, 1872 and 1882. Above, *circa* 1908, maintenance motorcar Number 100 crosses the Water Street Bridge towing a cargo of workers and materials. In 1912, the Union Traction operated three electric streetcar lines and carried an estimated one million passengers that year. The timber breaks seen in the lower photo protected the bridge pilings from being swept away by winter logjams. [*California History Room, California State Library, Sacramento, California*]

LATER BRIDGES: In 1908, the Union Traction Company built the three-hinge reinforced concrete bridge seen in the photo above. This bridge ran parallel to the Water Street Bridge to accommodate the newly built streetcar lines. [*California History Room, California State Library, Sacramento*] Over time, portions of the bridge were added, and lanes reconfigured until 1996, when the bridge underwent a major earthquake retrofit. Below, an art installation entitled "Fishing Rods," created by Nielsen Design Studies, decorates the north side of the current bridge. [*SBSL*]

FIRST MUNICIPAL BUILDINGS: After three previous locations, the county built the first dedicated courthouse seen in the above photo at right on Cooper Street in 1866. The City Hall shown at left was added in 1877 and the eight-sided Hall of Records in 1882. The devastating downtown fire of 1894 destroyed the first courthouse and in 1895, officials commissioned a new courthouse. [*Santa Cruz Museum of Art and History*] The photo below depicts today's view with only the Hall of Records remaining. The Latin phrase "*Sine Praejudicio*" translates to "without prejudice" and is the official motto of Santa Cruz County. [*SBSL*]

COURTHOUSE TO COOPER HOUSE: The handsome two-story Richardsonian Romanesque Revival building seen at top right replaced the old courthouse destroyed by fire. [*Santa Cruz Museum of Art and History*] With the courthouse moving across the river to a new government complex, developer Max Walden bought the old building in 1970 and remodeled it into the Cooper House, an eclectic mixture of shops, restaurants and bars. Beloved by residents and visitors alike, the building seemed to reflect the best qualities of Santa Cruz: colorful, vibrant and welcoming. Unfortunately, the 1989 earthquake damaged the building and it was demolished. Shown below, outdoor patio seating at a Cooper House restaurant. [*Santa Cruz Public Libraries, Marilyn Barrett*]

COUNTY BUILDINGS: Above, a county clerk sits at his desk surrounded by county maps and records (circa 1890s). [*Santa Cruz Museum of Art and History*] Below, the present Santa Cruz County Government Building with the Santa Cruz Courthouse, located to the right. The 1967 dedication and open-house ceremonies for the new building featured a colorful "Pageant of Pioneers" parade directed by Warren "Skip" Littlefield. Today the five-story building designed in the brutalist style with exposed concrete and ductwork houses a myriad of County Departments from the Assessor's Office to the County Treasurer. [*SBSL*]

COUNTY POOR FARM AND HOSPITAL: Santa Cruz pioneer David Gharky provided a portion of the funds for a county Poor Farm built on a then-rural site off Emeline Street. As local needs grew, other faculties were added, including a two-story hospital in 1885, a larger hospital in 1925 and a new sixty-five-bed County Hospital in 1968. Changes in the Federal Medicaid Program forced the closing of the in-patient and emergency services in 1973. Finally, by 1983, the remaining mental health facilities were moved to Dominican Hospital. [*Santa Cruz Museum of Art and History*] Today, the facility houses outpatient clinics and various other Public Health services. [*SBSL*]

THE HIHN MANSION: When built in 1872, the Hihn house was said to be the largest and most elaborate residence built in Santa Cruz. The mansion occupied an entire city block bounded by Locust, Center, Church and Chestnut Streets. Notable features of the home included a skating rink, gymnasium, a natural-light picture gallery, an elevator, speaking tubes and telegraph wires. German-born Frederick Hihn became wealthy with his investments in lumber mills, real estate, banking, railroads and the local water system. Below, the gardens of the mansion were equally impressive and included many exotic plantings. [*Santa Cruz Museum of Art and History*]

SANTA CRUZ CITY HALL: In 1920, the need for additional space led the city of Santa Cruz to leave the Front Street location and lease the Hihn Mansion. In 1923, the city purchased the mansion and site for $25,000, making $400-a-month payments. By 1937, the building no longer fit the municipal needs and the mansion was torn down to make way for a new Monterey Colonial Revival style city hall. Shown below, in keeping with the heritage of the former Hihn gardens, the city hall grounds feature a rose garden on the north side and other rare trees and shrubs in the front garden. [*SBSL*]

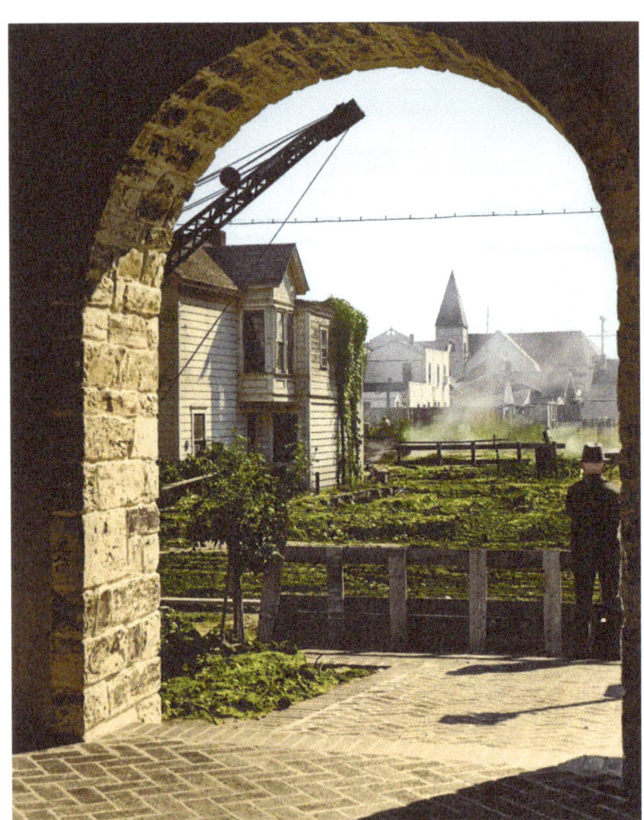

THE CIVIC AUDITORIUM: In 1940, voters approved a bond measure to build a new City Hall, a multi-purpose auditorium and a new fire station. The 2,000-seat Civic Auditorium was the site of the annual Miss California Beauty pageant until 1985, and has hosted many diverse entertainers, celebrities and special events over the years. In the photo above, a spectator watches as bulldozers clear the civic auditorium site in preparation for building. [*Special Collections, University Library, University of California, Santa Cruz, Historic Photos*] Below is the current view from city hall of the Civic Auditorium. [*SBSL*]

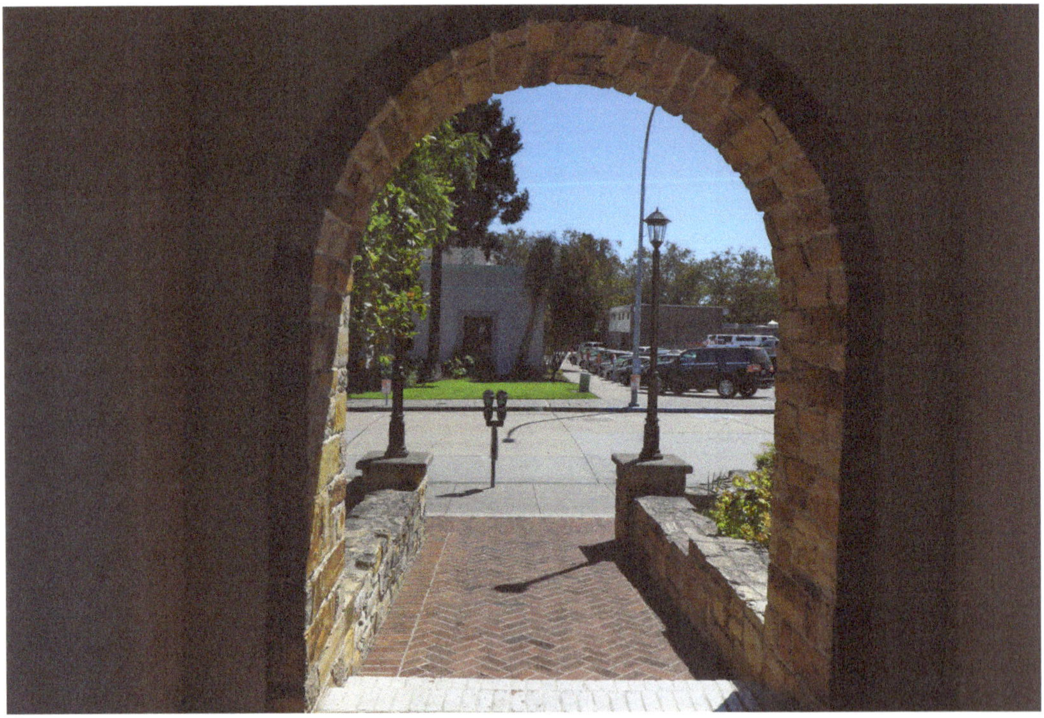

THE SANTA CRUZ LIBRARY: Early city founders recognized the importance of education and reading. A Library Association formed in 1868 with a reading room located in a downtown store and dues of $6.00 per year. The first public library opened in 1882 on the second floor of City Hall with books donated from the Library Association. Helped by a personal visit from Samuel Leask, Andrew Carnegie donated grants to help in the construction of four libraries, Santa Cruz main, Seabright, Soquel Avenue and Garfield Park. Shown above is the Carnegie Library built on Church Street in 1904. [*Ronnie Trubek*] Below, the present library built in 1968 replaced the Carnegie Library. [*SBSL*]

The Branciforte School: The earliest school on the Soquel Avenue site started out as a simple two-room building built in 1868. In the early days of the school, students recalled Principal William T. Forsythe (nicknamed "forty-eyes"), who required the pupils to march in formation to the classrooms each morning accompanied by the beating of a drum. Due to increasing student enrollment, a new Branciforte School was constructed in 1913 on the corner of Branciforte and Water Street. [*Santa Cruz Museum of Art and History*] Below, the present day Branciforte School now houses four alternative education schools and a Head Start Program. [*SBSL*]

BRANCIFORTE PLAZA: In 1929, a group of local doctors recognized the need for a local modern hospital and built Santa Cruz Hospital on the former Branciforte School site. The new hospital featured many modern amenities for the time such as gurney-sized elevators, x-ray and stereoscope machines, a cystoscopy table, a telephone switchboard connected to each room and a dumb waiter to carry food trays. [*Santa Cruz Museum of Art and History*] In 1949, the Adrian Dominican Sisters purchased the former Doctor's Hospital to replace their aging facility on West Cliff Drive. After eighteen years, the sisters moved to the newly built Dominican Hospital on Soquel Avenue. In 1976, the old hospital was sold and remodeled for commercial use. [*SBSL*]

MISSION HILL GRAMMAR SCHOOL: In 1857, an optimistic combination of taxes, subscriptions and promissory notes financed the first public school in Santa Cruz, a modest one-room building on Mission Hill. Increasing enrollment led to the building of a three-story building with an elevated basement in 1879. The 1906 earthquake left the building unstable and the upper floor and tower were removed. A 1928, a report critical of the safety of the old building caused the school board to vote to abandon the building and build a new school on nearby King Street. [*Santa Cruz Museum of Art and History*] Below, an office building has been built on the old school site; however, the rock steps and retaining wall remain. [*Author*]

 In the above image *circa* 1900, students in Miss Cox's fifth grade class at Mission Hill School pause their studies for a classroom photo. Note the wood stove to the left, the portrait of George Washington underneath the flag and the large expanses of blackboard. [*Santa Cruz Museum of Art and History*] The lower photo depicts the Santa Cruz Public Library of the 1890s, located in the Hotaling Building, which was later remodeled into the St. George Hotel. Head librarian Miss Minerva Waterman is seated to the left and a Mr. Cox is seated to the right. [*Santa Cruz Public Libraries*]

SANTA CRUZ HIGH: The first public high school in Santa Cruz occupied the top floor of the Mission Hill School until the first dedicated high school opened in 1897 on Walnut Street. In 1913, the school caught fire and burned to the ground, but was rebuilt in 1915 with twenty-seven classrooms and an 830-seat auditorium. [*Santa Cruz Museum of Art and History*] The first graduating class of 1878 consisted of four students. In contrast, the current total enrollment at Santa Cruz High runs around 1,100 students per year. [*SBSL*]

5

SURF CITY, SANTA CRUZ

A woman stands on the ocean-side bluff with an early view of the Museum, Vieu de L'Eau Station and Arch Rock behind her. [*Ronnie Trubek*]

VIEU DE L'EAU: The trolley line carried tourists down Garfield Avenue (now Woodrow Avenue) to the last stop at West Cliff Drive. Visitors to the pagoda-style station could go up to the second-story observatory, dance or dine at the nearby casino (seen in the upper photo at right) or view the exhibits of sea mosses, shells and birds at the nearby museum. [*Santa Cruz Museum of Art and History*] Above in this present-day view, the empty streetcar right-of-way down Woodrow Avenue can still be seen. [*SBSL*]

THE SANTA CRUZ LIGHTHOUSE: Early pioneer Adna Hecox operated the first lighthouse built on the cliffs near the Vieu de L'Eau. When Hecox retired, his daughter, Laura, took over his duties for the next thirty-three years. Her vast collection of marine specimens, minerals and Indian baskets became the nucleus of the Santa Cruz Natural History Museum. [*Santa Cruz Museum of Art and History*] By 1948, the lighthouse was no longer needed and torn down. Above, in 1967, Chuck and Esther Abbot built a replica lighthouse as a memorial to their son lost in a bodysurfing accident. The building is now a surfing museum and the adjacent grounds overlook Steamer Lane, a popular surfing spot. [*SBSL*]

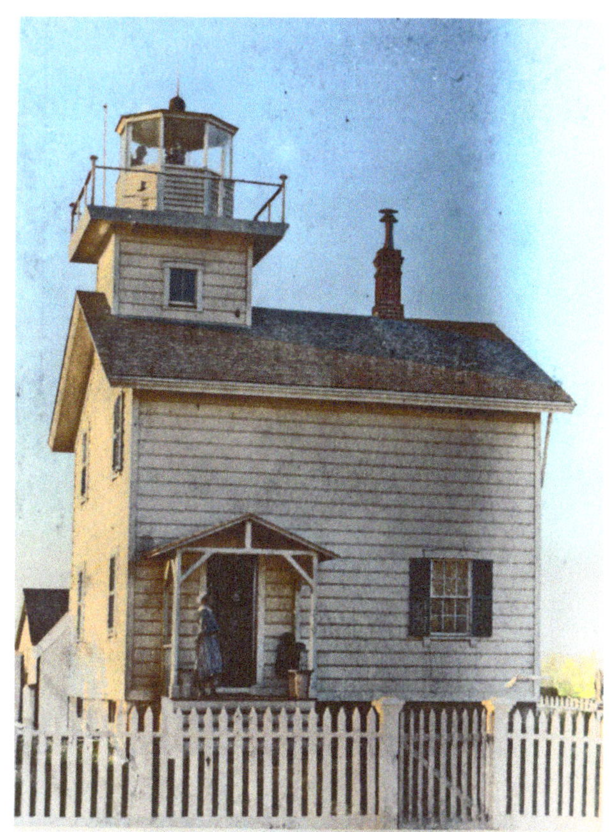

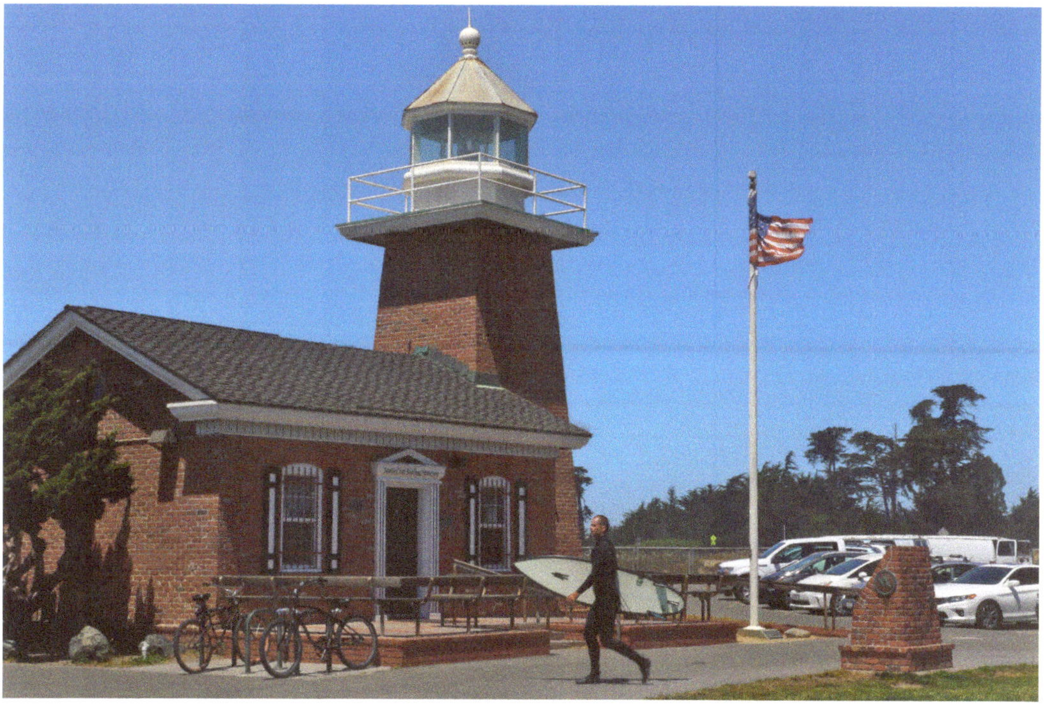

DE LAVEAGA ZOO AND PARK: In 1894, wealthy businessman José Vincente de Laveaga passed away. Profoundly deaf his whole life, he left a provision in his will for a home for the physically challenged to be built on a portion of his ranch in the Santa Cruz foothills. However, relatives contested the will and in the final settlement, de Laveaga's 565-acre ranch became a public park. Seen above, families enjoy the park reached by streetcar up Morrissey Avenue. [*Santa Cruz Museum of Art and History, Ole Ravnos*] Below, around 1912, the city constructed a small zoo containing Jumbo the buffalo, Jocko the spider monkey, bears, elk, deer, a fox and a raccoon. The zoo closed in 1933. [*Santa Cruz Museum of Art and History*]

MORE DE LAVEAGA HISTORY: Following a nation-wide boom in oil exploration, the Laveaga Trust Oil Company installed an exploratory oil derrick seen above, at the eastern end of De Laveaga Park in 1923. After a few years, the well proved unprofitable and the oil company folded. [*Santa Cruz Museum of Art and History*] Sadly, there are few remnants of the old zoo today. A few pieces of the original entrance shown in the photo below are located just off Prospect Heights. [*SBSL*]

WOOD'S LAGOON: The need for a local protected harbor became evident when a 1959 storm damaged thirty-one boats. Above, in 1964, bulldozers began moving earth to transform the former Wood's Lagoon into the Santa Cruz Small Craft Harbor. [*Santa Cruz Museum of Art and History*] When dedicated in 1964, there were only 360 boat slips; today, that number has grown to 1,475 spaces. [*SBSL*] In 1992, a coalition of efforts led to the establishment the Monterey Bay National Marine Sanctuary. This federally protected marine area stretches south from Rocky Point (just north of San Francisco), then south along the coast through Santa Cruz County and ends in the town of Cambria in San Luis Obispo County.

Acknowledgments

First and foremost, I would like to thank Siân Burckett St. Laurent, the "present day" photographer for this book. It has been a pleasure working with you, both on a professional and personal level. I hope you have enjoyed the adventure as much as I have, despite our "problems" with fog, telephone and power lines, traffic, sand flies and even too many trees. Secondly, I would like to thank my family, friends and colleagues for supplying photos from their collections and listening to my endless discourses on Santa Cruz history. Special thanks to Ross Eric Gibson for reading my manuscript and suggesting appropriate edits and corrections. However, any mistakes found in this publication are strictly the work of the author and any corrections should be directed to the author at debbie.muth@sbcglobal.net.

A big thank you to those who supplied photos for the book: Marla Novo, the Santa Cruz Museum of Art and History; Luisa Haddad, University Library, University of California, Santa Cruz; Deborah Lipoma, Santa Cruz County Libraries; Jessie Durant, Ted Whiting III and Brigid Fuller of the Santa Cruz Beach Boardwalk; Charlene Duval, Sourisscau Academy for State and Local History, San Jose State University; Library of Congress, Washington, D.C.; California State Library, Sacramento, California; The Society of California Pioneers, San Francisco; Ronnie Trubek, the Fine Arts Museums of San Francisco; Wendy Brannan, Dana Bagshaw, Calvary Episcopal Church, Santa Cruz; Corbett Wright; and History San José.

Finally, to the readers: I hope this book sparks your interest in Santa Cruz history and encourages further research on your part.

FURTHER READING

Print

An Architectural Tour of Historic Santa Cruz County, Allan Allen and Ross Eric Gibson
California Central Coast Railways, Rick Hamman
Chinese Gold: The Chinese in the Monterey Bay Region, Sandy Lydon
"Como la sombra huye la hora," Restoration Research, Santa Cruz Mission Adobe,
    Santa Cruz Mission State Park, Edna Kimbra, et. al.
The Leftmost City, Power and Progressive Politics in Santa Cruz, Richard Gendrom and
    G. William Domhoff
Lime Kiln Legacies: The History of the Lime Industry in Santa Cruz County, Frank Perry, et. al.
The Santa Cruz Beach Boardwalk: A Century by the Sea, The Santa Cruz Seaside Company
The Sidewalk Companion to Santa Cruz Architecture, John Leighton Chase, et al.
Surf, Sand and Streetcars: A Mobile History of Santa Cruz, California, Charles McCaleb.

Internet

Santa Cruz Public Library: www.santacruzpl.org
Santa Cruz Beach Boardwalk: www.beachboardwalk.com
Santa Cruz Museum of Art and History—History blogs: www.santacruzmah.org/blog
Fun Facts: www.researchersanonymous.weebly.com/fun-stuff.html

To Visit

Santa Cruz Museum of Art and History: 705 Front Street, Santa Cruz, 95060,
www.santacruzmah.org

Santa Cruz Mission State Historical Park:
www.thatsmypark.org/parks-and-beaches/santa-cruz-mission-state-historic-park